THE TEENS GUIDE TO STARTING YOUR OWN BUSINESS

Your Step by Step Blueprint to Becoming a Teen Entrepreneur

Tanya Rogers
David Rogers

Rogers Publishing

Copyright © 2020 David Rogers

All rights reserved

Selling For Kids Book Series
Volume 1 - The Kids Guide To Selling: How I was Able To Make $4,000 in 60 Days

Volume 2 - The Teens Guide To Starting Your Own Business: Your Step by Step Blueprint to Becoming a Teen Entrepreneur

Volume 3 – The Teens Guide to Becoming an Entrepreneur: 102 Ways That You Can Start to Think Like a Successful Entrepreneur.

Volume 4 – The Teens Guide to Mastering Sales: How You Need to Think to Become Successful at Selling

No part of this book may be reproduced, or stored in a retrieval system, or transmitted in any form or by any means, electronic, mechanical, photocopying, recording, or otherwise, without express written permission of the publisher.

We can not guarantee that your results will be the same as the author's. This material is for educational purposes only.

Cover design by: David Rogers
Printed in the United States of America

CONTENTS

Title Page
Copyright
How to Get the Most From this Book
Introduction
Chapter 1: What is an Entrepreneur? — 1
Chapter 2: What Kind Of Business To Start — 8
Chapter 3: Initial Investment — 13
Chapter 4: How To Reinvest — 21
Chapter 5: Why You Need To Save — 27
Chapter 6: Explore New Products — 34
Chapter 7: Take Action Now — 41
Chapter 8: Step by Step Blueprint — 46
Sign Up For The Selling For Kids Newsletter — 57
About The Author — 59
About The Author — 61
Books In This Series — 63
Follow Us — 65

HOW TO GET THE MOST FROM THIS BOOK

Step #1: Register Your Copy Of The Teens Guide To Starting Your Own Business For Free

When you register, you will get exclusive access to Advance Reader Copies of future releases, offers, discounts, plus tips and training.

Click Here to register or

Go to >> SellingForKids.com/Business

Step #2: Read The Entire Book And Then Take Immediate Action

We created this book so that it can be read quickly and you can get started as soon as possible. Don't delay and get started on your journey today.

INTRODUCTION

Welcome to the second book in our Selling for Kids Book Series, *The Teens Guide to Starting Your Own Business: Your Step by Step Blueprint to Becoming a Teen Entrepreneur*. Don't let the name fool you though, our material is for Teens, Pre-Teens, Children, and adults too. You're never too young or too old to learn about entrepreneurship or success.

While there are other books out there that can teach you about entrepreneurship or give you 50 different business ideas that you can start as a kid or teen. We haven't seen any that will give you an exact blueprint that you can use to start making money right away. That's why we decided to create the Selling for Kids Book series, so that we can help as many "kids" as possible begin their first business and start generating an income as soon as they're done reading it.

In this book, we will be going over each step of the blueprint that will allow you to start your own business and start generating income right away. In fact, this is the blueprint I used to $4,000 in 60 days.

Here are some things you will learn about:

   -First, we will tell you what we think an entrepreneur is and why you should become one.

-Next, we are going to cover what type of business model you should start (hint: it's the one we teach you about in The Kids Guide to Selling)

-We will also be teaching you about your initial investment using startup capital.

-Then we will teach about reinvesting so that you can continue to grow your business.

-After that, we will explain how to save money for your goals.

-Then we'll go into how to explore and test new products to sell.

-The next part will be about the different levels of taking action.

-Lastly, we will give you the exact blueprint that you can use to start selling right away and start creating an income for you to achieve your goals.

We always try to keep our ideas simple and easy to understand. We want you to be able to get as much as you can from what you've read. But if at any point you have questions, you can reach out to us at our website:

sellingforkids.com

Now, let's start out by discussing what exactly is an entrepreneur and why you choose this path.

CHAPTER 1: WHAT IS AN ENTREPRENEUR?

"This doesn't have to be complicated. You are an entrepreneur when you start working for yourself!"

- DAVID ROGERS

We hear the word entrepreneur thrown around a lot, but what exactly does it mean to be an entrepreneur? Let's start by answering that question.

Let's look at what Wikipedia says.

> An **entrepreneur** is an individual who creates a new business, bearing most of the risks and enjoying most of the rewards. The process of setting up a business is known as entrepreneurship. The entrepreneur is commonly seen as an innovator, a source of new ideas, goods, services, and business/or procedures.

I definitely think an entrepreneur can be all of these things. The way I see it is a little simpler than their definition. I believe you are an *entrepreneur* when you begin to work for **yourself** and not others.

Let's look at some examples of what I mean when I say this.

> You are 16 years old, and you open a lemonade stand and sell lemonade. I believe you're an entrepreneur.

> But let's say you were 16 years old and you went to work for a store at the mall that sells lemonade. You are not an entrepreneur, and you're an employee.

Let's look at another example.

> You go to medical school and become a doctor. After you graduate, you work at a local hospital. Then you would not be an entrepreneur, and you'd be an employee.

> However, after graduating from medical school, you open your *own* doctor's office. In this case, you would be an entrepreneur.

In both these cases, regardless of age or education level, you are an entrepreneur when you work for yourself. Even if you are just a young hustler or someone like a doctor, you can be an entrepreneur or an employee.

9 To 5 Or Entrepreneur

In your life, you are going to have to make a choice. On the one hand, you'll have the opportunity to get your degree and work for someone else's company. But on the other hand, you can still get your degree and start your own company. The choice is yours.

Now I don't know if you plan on getting a degree or not, and it doesn't really matter because either way, you'll still have to make that choice, to either be an employee or an entrepreneur.

Many people feel you have more security when working for someone else or a big corporation. People like to have that steady paycheck and medical benefits that come with being an employee.

But there is another group of people that feel the opposite way. They think they have more security when working for themselves and not under someone else's rule. They like the feeling of being able to provide for themselves and be in control of their own destiny.

What Are Some Reasons People Choose Entrepreneurship?

There are thousands of reasons to take that giant step and become an entrepreneur.

Here are just a few of them:

> **Autonomy** – The idea of running your own business allows you to be in charge of your destiny, and it can help you avoid getting stuck in the "daily grind," or as Rich Dad Poor Dad's author Robert Kiyosaki puts it, the "rat race." Running their own business lets, many entrepreneurs have a self-

sustaining career.

Opportunity – By becoming an entrepreneur, you will open up a whole new world of opportunity. You will have the chance to do anything that you want in life. Being an entrepreneur gives you the ability to either create real change in the world or live the life you dreamed about. Few other career choices are available that can offer this kind of opportunity.

Impact – Many people want to help their employers or company be successful, but few can make such an impact. When running your own business, everything you do will directly impact the company, which can be very rewarding.

Freedom - This is easily the answer most people will give you if asked why they want to become entrepreneurs. Being able to do what they want and when they want to is the driving reason behind taking the risk of running their own business. It is true, and having freedom in life and career does make a huge difference!

Responsibility - When running your own business, you can run it the way you feel it should be. This is especially true if you wish to help other people. When you work for someone else, you may not have the ability to help the world the way you would like to, but you can if you are the boss.

Be your Own Boss - This is another big reason people have for becoming entrepreneurs. When you are the boss, you can do things your way, and you can decide your own fate by making your own decisions or taking your own risks.

Time and Family – When you have created a self-sustaining company, being an entrepreneur could give you freedom and time, allowing you to spend more of it with your family. It could also allow you to make your family a part of your company, something you can't do when working for someone else.

Create a Legacy - If the idea of creating a lasting legacy is important to you, very few careers allow you to do so, like operating your own business. Imagine if you were to start a company that could impact millions of people's lives and does it for generations.

Accomplishment - If there are specific goals you would like to accomplish in your life, running your own business could help you get there.

Control - For many business owners, the sense of security that comes with controlling your work or destiny is a primary reason to become an entrepreneur.

Now that we covered why you should become an entrepreneur let's look at what it takes to become an entrepreneur.

How Do I Get Started As An Entrepreneur?

Becoming an entrepreneur may seem like an enormous task and

something that you need to have many skills to do. However, in this book, we will focus on the **easiest, *fastest*, and least expensive way to get started**. In fact, you can get started for as little as **one dollar**.

Your first step into entrepreneurship isn't going to be creating the next Apple or Amazon. It's going to be something small but profitable. As we said, you are an entrepreneur when you begin to work for yourself, and that's why *selling* is the easiest way to get started. Many people may not see this as the first step of entrepreneurship, but we believe it is essential to getting started.

We will guide you through this process step-by-step and show you how selling is a way to generate significant income while also learning what it takes to move to the next level of entrepreneurship.

There are a couple of things you need to get started in entrepreneurship. The first is you need to have the right mindset. And the second is that you need to have a plan. In this book, we will help you with both of these.

In the next chapter, I'll explain what are the different types of business models you can start. Of course, we will be using the business model from The Kids Guide to Selling. Also, since this book is an expansion of the first book, I do recommend giving it a read to make following along easier.

However, if you haven't, that's ok too. Just by using this book as your guide, you should have no trouble starting this business.

Chapter 1 Questions

1) When are you considered to be an entrepreneur?

2) What would you prefer to be, an employee or an entrepreneur?

3) What are some reasons you choose the answer to the previous question?

4) Since we are going to show you the easiest, fastest and least expensive way to get started as an entrepreneur. Is there any other reason why you wouldn't get started right now?

CHAPTER 2: WHAT KIND OF BUSINESS TO START

"You don't start a business, you are a business"

- GRANT CARDONE

All right, so now you know the some of the reasons why people choose entrepreneurship. Now we're going to look at what vehicle you're going to use to reach those goals. Of course, when we say the vehicle, we mean what kind of business you're going to start.

For the purpose of this book, we have a specific type of business model we are implementing. However, we think it's a good idea to cover some examples of the two different business models you can choose from. So in the next couple of chapters, we'll be giving examples of both.

Selling Vs Services

As we mentioned already, there are two different types of business models you can choose from. The first one is **selling**, and the second one is **services**. Now technically both of these business models require selling. In the first one, you are selling a product or *item*. With the second one, you are selling your services that you will provide to your customer.

Let's take a look at the four following scenarios and see if you can determine the best two of them.

Scenario 1: Selling

After going to a yard sale you find 10 video games for a really good deal. You buy them and resell them on eBay for $10 each. After a few days you have sold them all and you make $100 in sales.

Scenario 2: Services

You go around to all your neighbors and ask them to let you mow their lawns. You tell them that you are great at it and will only charge them $25 a week for letting you take care of this for them. Two of your neighbors like the sound of this offer and agree to let you do this for them. You are now generating $200 a month in sales.

Scenario 3: Selling

You buy a case of candy bars from your local Dollar Tree. Then you resell them individually to customers for $3 each.

After about two hours of selling, you are done with the case and your total sales are $108.

Scenario 4: Services

You go visit some local restaurants in your city. You then pitch the owner of the restaurant about handling all their social media accounts for them. You let them know how you will post on their social media three times a day, every day of the month and it will only cost them $500 a month. The restaurant owner likes what you offer and signs a 12-month contract. You now have a sale for $6000 for a year of social media management.

Can you spot what the **best** two scenarios are from above?

If you answered numbers 3 and 4, you'd be correct.

The Fastest Path To Cash

In scenario three, you achieve what we call the **"Fastest Path to Cash."** What the fastest path to cash means is what can you do right now that will allow you to generate cash the quickest. In scenario three you are able to generate **$100+** in the shortest amount of time possible, generally between one to two hours.

However, with scenario four you are able to generate a lot of cash by selling just one service for a year. You are able to make *recurring income* which is an entrepreneur's dream. This scenario would actually rank number two for the fastest path to cash though. This is because it requires learning a skill to perform it versus just buying something and selling it.

The service in scenario four is what's called **Digital Marketing** or **Internet Marketing**. Digital marketing can include many different services. Social media management is just one type of service that can be provided. As you can see by how much a 12-month contract can be worth, this can be a very profitable type of service to provide.

In this book, we will not be covering these kinds of services. This topic really requires a book of its own. So be on the lookout, we may have one coming out pretty soon.

Now that we understand the two main types of businesses available to choose from. Let's start taking a look at what **Capital** (*money*) is needed to start your business and where to find it. Remember, we said you can start our business model for just a dollar.

Chapter 2 Questions

1) We spoke about two business models, selling and services. Which business model are you going to start?

2) Why are you choosing to start the business model you selected from the question above?

3) We also told you about "The fastest path to cash." Describe what that means to you.

4) The last thing we talked about was internet marketing (or digital marketing.) Is this something you would be interested in learning more about? Sign up to our newsletter **HERE** or go to **sellingforkids.com** and we will let you know when this training is available.

CHAPTER 3: INITIAL INVESTMENT

"I knew that if I failed, I wouldn't regret that, but I knew the one thing I might regret is not trying."

--JEFF BEZOS, FOUNDER AND CEO OF AMAZON

The first thing that you will need to do to start this process is to make your initial investment. You are going to need what's called "startup capital". Most new businesses need to have this to begin making their product or service available for customers, and your business is no different.

What Is Startup Capital?

So, what exactly is startup capital? Let's take a look.

Startup capital is the money that it will take to launch or start your business or service. It can be used to pay for office space, equipment, inventory, and many other things.

For example, if you were to start a lawnmowing service in your neighborhood. You would need money to purchase a lawn mower, weed eater, edger, and some gasoline for your equipment. Also, you might need money to make copies of flyers to hand out to neighbors, or to print business cards. These are just some ideas of what you may need startup capital (money) for.

How Much Startup Capital Do I Need?

How much you'll need is going to depend on what type of business or service you are going to provide. As we covered in *The Kids Guide to Selling*, you will need to decide on a product (or service) you are going to provide and then you can determine just how much money you will need to start.

Let's look at the lawnmowing service example again. Let's say you want to start that business and you needed to purchase all the equipment from the previous example. You check on Craigslist because you want to start with as little money as possible. You find that the lawn mower is $50, the weed eater is also $50. But you find someone who is moving and giving away an edger for free.

You can get the three main pieces of equipment that you'll need for only $100. However, you'll also need to let people know about your service. You create a flyer and plan to print $50 worth of copies to hand out to your neighbors. So, you are now looking at $150 to launch your new lawnmowing service. This is what your startup capital will need to be, $150.

Luckily the business model we are going to discuss here in this book has a really low startup cost. I'll be using $30 as the startup cost in this book because it is what I started out with. But you are free to choose a different amount.

Where Do I Get Startup Capital?

Typically, this will be money that you already have saved. We will be using that money to make our initial investment in your new business. Since you know what your startup costs are, you can simply get that saved money and go purchase what you need.

"But wait a minute! I don't have any money saved!" Don't worry, we are about to cover what you can do if you don't have any money saved already. There are a few different ways you can do this.

No Money, No Problem

The first thing you can do is to ask someone in your family for a loan to let you get started. Typically, your family believes in you the most and would love to support your ideas. You simply go up to them and explain what your new business idea is. After you explain it to them, you can ask them if they would be able to help you get started by loaning you the amount of money that you need.

How To Ask Family

Let's take a look at an example of how I would ask for the startup capital for the lawnmowing service.

> *Hey mom, I need to ask you a question. Do you have a minute? Mom, you know how I want to go on my schools' field trip to Washington D.C.? Well, I have an idea of how I can raise the money to go. And as a bonus, you won't have to pay for any of the $1,000 cost yourself! Would you like to hear more about my idea? Great, let me explain. I want to raise the money for the trip by mowing lawns for the next 9 weeks.*

Then I would continue to explain the exact details of my plan. After I explained the plan, then I would ask this.

> *Mom, now that you understand what my plan is and how it won't cost you anything. Can I ask you one small favor so I can get started on this plan? I need to borrow $150 to get the equipment I need to start the lawn service. I would only be borrowing the money and then I will pay you back in full in exactly 2 weeks. Can I get your help with this?*

And that's it! Done. Most of the time this is all it will probably take. However, keep in mind that many times your parents may not have this money extra or available. There is a study that's out that says 76% of households in America are living paycheck to paycheck. So, there is a good chance that your household maybe this way. And if it is, don't worry about it, there are other ways to get money to start your new business.

Friends And Neighbors Can Help Too

Asking your friends and neighbors are the next best groups of people to ask for help from. They will usually support your ideas and would like to see you succeed as well. Just as you asked your family for help by pitching them your idea, you will do the same with your friends and neighbors.

The worst that can happen is that they tell you "no". That's it. If they say no, simply go to the next person you know and pitch them your idea as well. Someone telling you "no" is not the end of the world. And remember, 76% of households are living paycheck to paycheck, this includes your friends and neighbors too. Don't look at them negatively if they can't help. Besides, there are still more ways to get your startup capital!

No Money, No Help, Now What?

It's time for some decisions to be made. You have a goal of how much money you need to start your new business. However, you don't have any funding sources. What can you do?

Here's the first idea. Take a look at what you need and see if there is anything you can do to work around it.

Going back to the lawnmowing service idea. Do you have any family, friends, or neighbors that have the equipment you need? I'd bet there is a good chance that you will know someone that has a lawn mower, weed eater, or edger. You can even go up to them and simply ask if you can borrow their item from them.

Be Willing To Work Out A Deal

Maybe you can even work out a deal where you will do their lawn for free for allowing you to use their equipment. This way, you eliminate the needed startup capital and still get to earn the money you need by using someone else's equipment. Something to think about when using someone else's equipment though. If it breaks down while you're using it, it's going to be your responsibility to pay for it to be fixed or repaired.

No One To Borrow Equipment From, Try This

There are still a few more things that we can do to get the needed startup capital.

The next thing you could try is to start recycling bottles and cans. Now not all states have recycling redemption values. So, you'll need to see if your city/state has this program. If they do, awesome, we can get started.

The easiest way to do this is similar to asking for a loan. You can go to your family, friends, and neighbors and ask them to please save all their recycling for you. Let them know what your business plan is and that you are going to raise the startup capital that you need by collecting items to recycle.

You can go by their place once a week, or every two weeks and pick up the recyclable items they have saved for you. Recyclable items can add up fast, so you will probably make the needed startup capital pretty quickly.

Here's Your Last Strategy To Get The Startup Capital

If you are at this point and you haven't been able to get the needed startup capital, there's one more thing to try.

Get ONE DOLLAR from someone, just one dollar. With this one dollar, I would be able to get the needed $150 startup capital from our example lawnmowing service idea in less than 2 hours!

I will explain how I, and you, can do this in the last chapter of this book. It's pretty easy.

Chapter 3 Questions

1) What is startup capital?

2) Why do you need startup capital?

3) What are some ways you can get startup capital if you don't have any?

4) How will you ask for startup capital? What is your "pitch"?

5) What is your last option for startup capital? How much money do you need?

CHAPTER 4: HOW TO REINVEST

"Your Greatness is limited only by the investments you make in yourself."

--GRANT CARDONE

Now the next step to this process is to keep reinvesting the income you are generating. If you are making money, then you are probably selling something whether it's an actual product or a service. If it's a product, you'll need to reinvest in more products. If it's a service, then you may need to reinvest in additional equipment.

What Does Reinvest Mean?

Let's take a look at what it means to reinvest.

Reinvest means that you are taking the profits from your

sales and purchasing more merchandise or equipment to continue promoting your business.

In other words, you are not making money and then just keeping it for yourself. You are using it to continue growing your business. Remember that you are creating a business and you need to treat it like a business. You will want to continue with this strategy of reinvesting as long as you can.

Let's Look At An Example Of Reinvesting.

This time let's say we started selling video games on eBay. We got our startup capital and purchased 10 games from the swap meet (flea market). You listed them on eBay and sold 2 games on your first day. Let's say you purchased the games for $5 each and sold them for $25 each. Your profit is $40 for both games.

Now you take the $40 and go back to the swap meet and purchase 8 more video games at $5 each. You come back home and then you list the new games. Let's say you sell 3 games on your second day and you make a $60 profit. Now you will take the $60 profit and go back to the swap meet again and this time you purchase 12 video games at $5 each.

So, let's look at this. You made a total of $100 profit ($40 + $60). You reinvested all $100 back into your business by purchasing more inventory. You started with an inventory of 10 video games, and now you have 25 video games after reinvesting.

This is the basic idea of reinvesting. You will be using a little more strategy when you reinvest your money back into your business.

We will give you the exact blueprint of this strategy in the last chapter, but this example gives us a good idea of how it works.

Why Do I Need To Keep Reinvesting?

Reinvesting is crucial to your business. If you aren't reinvesting, then you are probably spending. And spending will most likely lead to the failure of your business. Now it is said that we learn from our failures, but I don't want you to fail when I'm telling you what to do so you don't fail on something simple like this.

The only way that you can continue to grow your business is by purchasing more products to sell or any new equipment that may be needed for performing a service.

What Not To Do

Let's imagine in the eBay seller example. You sell the first 2 video games on the first day. You make a $40 profit and say "yeah! I got 40 bucks" and then you go to the store and purchase $40 on "stuff", not reinvesting your profit. Then the second day, let's say you still sell 3 video games and make a $60 profit. You have another "yeah" moment and decide to go to the mall and spend $60 on a new shirt.

Now we'll assume that a couple more days go by and you don't make any sales, it happens. Then on the fifth day, you make 4 more sales. Cool, $80 in profit. You think for a moment about reinvesting in more products but decide it's better to keep it safe by keeping it in your wallet, you know, "just in case." After all, you're not going to spend it. You're just going to hold it just in case of an emergency.

A couple more day's pass by and you finally make another sale on eBay! Awesome, oh but wait, that was my last game. I need to go buy more. You open your wallet and only see three dollars in there. Wait a minute, I had $80! Then you realize that you actually spent that money slowly over the past few days and didn't even notice that it was getting low.

This is just an example, but believe me, it happens just like this all the time.

I Borrowed My Initial Money

Now the only thing that you want to do before reinvesting is if you borrowed your startup capital from someone, you'll want to pay them back as soon as possible. So, this should be one of your priorities after you start earning income. However, make sure you still have enough to reinvest some of it back into your business.

In the two examples I've given so far, the lawnmowing service and the eBay seller, the startup costs would be $50 or more. However, just remember coming in the last chapter, I'm going to show you how you can do this with only $1. So, if you simply borrowed $1, that will be very easy to payback.

Never Run Out Of Product

Another part of reinvesting will be keeping a certain amount of inventory in your possession. In other words, part of your profit will need to go towards purchasing more products.

Looking back at the eBay seller example you can see that when you don't reinvest your money into products you will have a higher chance of spending it and not having any product left to sell. So, you must make it a discipline to use part of your money to purchase more items for resale.

In a later chapter, will be going into more detail about this idea. But for now, just think of it this way. If you have a product that you are selling very well, you don't want to ever run out of that product. Because, even if you run out of money but you still have a product, you can always make more money again.

Chapter 4 Questions

1) What does it mean to Reinvest?

2) What will happen to your business if you reinvest into it?

(Fill in the blank)
3) And _____ will most likely lead to the failure of your business.

4) What should you Never do with your product?

CHAPTER 5: WHY YOU NEED TO SAVE

"It's not how much money you make, but how much you keep, how hard it works for you, and how many generations you keep it for."

--ROBERT KIYOSAKI

We are going to be covering the topic of saving in this chapter. I have mentioned saving earlier in the book, but now we are going to be going deeper into this topic. This will be one of the most important parts of this process.

Why Do I Need To Save?

As we discussed in *The Kids Guide to Selling*, the number one thing you need to do is to set a goal. This is where you must start to know what direction you are going. If you haven't set a goal for yourself yet, you need to stop reading and set your goal. It's that important.

I gave the example in *The Kids Guide to Selling* that when I would sell and not have a goal, I would do terribly. One time in 4 hours I only made $20. However, there was another time that I wanted to go to Universal Studios Hollywood. I set my goal high enough to pay for mine and my brother's tickets and I was able to perform so much better.

Over 2 days, I made $500 selling. It ended up being enough money that I was able to buy us both annual passes to Universal instead of just single-day tickets. And timewise, it was only a few more hours than I spent to make the $20!

So once again, if you haven't set your goals yet, do it right away.

Move This Money To An Account Or Safe Location

Once you have your goals set, then you can start to figure out what to do with the income and profit you are generating. Just like any other business that is out there, you need to dedicate part of your profit to reinvest into your business and another part needs to go into savings. We'll call these savings your "Goal Money Fund" because this is where the money for achieving your goal will go.

Where your Goal Money Fund is located is completely up to you. You can set up a savings account at a local bank or credit union. Depending on your age you may need to have a parent or guardian help you out with this.

You can also find a safe place in your home to keep your money.

Just something to think about though, if your money is too easy to access, you run the risk of spending it instead of saving it. And of course, you could always have your parent or guardian save it for you as well.

Create An Emergency Fund

Another type of savings you may want to set up would be an Emergency Fund. This would be separate savings than the one you have set up for your Goal Money Fund. This would be a fund that you have some money set aside in to cover any last-minute expenses or bills you may get. This way you can cover those expenses without having to dip into your Goal Money Fund.

How much money you dedicate to this fund is completely up to you as well. I will usually just keep a couple of hundred dollars in mine. But as I get older and have more expenses, I know I will increase the amount that I keep in it.

How Much Money Should I Be Saving?

You need to save as much as possible, *after* reinvesting into your business. There isn't necessarily a right or wrong amount. This is another one of those things that will depend on your circumstances.

In the last chapter of this book, we will be going over the exact blueprint of how I made $4,000 in 60 days. In that chapter, I will also be telling you exactly how much to reinvest and how much to save based on my experience with this.

But you also need to know that your results may be different than mine. By the time I had done those kinds of sales I already had more than a year of selling experience. But there is no reason why you can't duplicate it yourself and do even better than I did.

Set A Baseline Of How Much To Save

Once you determine how much product you need to keep, remember that you never want to run out of a product. You can set a baseline of how much money you want to save.

Here is a general rule that you can use to help you. Keep in mind that this works best once you have enough product in your inventory.

Let's say that you are selling items that cost you $1 each, the same items from the last chapter that you are reselling for $3. Also, let's say that you want to keep a minimum of 20 of these with you. So, you start your day with 20 exactly. Throughout the day you sell 15 of them and end up making $45, and you have 5 items left.

The first thing you will need to do is to purchase 15 of these items again to make up for what you sold. So, you spend $15 on them. Now you have $30 left from the money you made. I would take all of the $30 and put it into my Goal Money Fund.

Do you see how I reinvested the same amount that I used? I sold 15, then I bought 15 to replace them. The money that was left could now be saved because it's what was left over after I reinvested into my business.

Keep Saving

So, to reemphasize this, you need to save as much as you can. You don't want to spend your money unless it gets you closer to your goal. What do I mean by this? To simply put it, only spend or invest your money in things that are going to help you get more sales or to help more people for service businesses.

Going back to the lawnmowing service business. If you are the only person that is doing the lawn work, buying a second lawnmower won't help you do more yards. It will not help you make more money.

But what if you bought a better lawnmower, maybe one that has a bag attached to it that will collect all the grass trimmings. This could potentially save you a lot of time that you would normally spend raking. You can now use that time you're saving to do a second yard each day. This could double the sales you make each day! and that would be awesome!

Keep Committed To Your Goals

If you have your goals set and are putting the money you earn towards them, you shouldn't have any problems with staying committed to doing what you are doing. As you see yourself get closer to your goal, you will get more excited and pumped up, your commitment should go up too.

This also why in *The Kids Guide to Selling* I recommended starting with smaller goals and then working up towards bigger ones. As you achieve all the smaller goals, you will get very excited, and you will gain valuable selling skills while doing them. This way when you have a big goal you want to hit; you will be better skilled, and it will be easier to achieve it.

Can I Spend Just A Little Bit?

You may be tempted to spend some of the money that you have earned up to this point. You need to make sure you think like a business owner and if you think you might be tempted to spend some of it, plan it out. When you are determining how much to reinvest and how much to save, go ahead, and set a certain amount aside to spend. Think of it like you're paying yourself a salary.

Although, I would not recommend that you do this right away. You need some time to get your reinvesting and savings figured out first. After you have these two things planned out, it will be easier to figure out an amount to keep for personal spending.

Chapter 5 Questions

1) Before you start, what is the number one thing you need to do?

2) Why is it important to save?

3) We talked about two kinds of savings. What are they called?

(fill in the blank)
4) You can set a _____ of how much money you want to save.

5) Can you spend just a little bit? Why or Why Not?

CHAPTER 6: EXPLORE NEW PRODUCTS

"I have not failed. I've just found 10,000 ways that won't work"

--THOMAS EDISON

We have gone over a lot of information so far. We've covered what the initial investment is and where we can get that startup capital. We've talked about the idea of reinvesting into our business and never running out of a product. Then we saw how we need to approach saving money so that we can hit our goals. And now the last part we are going to cover is about testing and exploring new products.

This is going to be a very important part of how you can grow your business. If you don't test new products to sell, you will be limiting your true potential.

I started my journey into selling by selling school fundraiser candy bars. If I wouldn't have tried different products, I wouldn't have been able to grow my business. The reason for this is because when I purchased these candy bars, I had a limited selection to choose from. There were typically only 4 or 5 flavors to choose from.

Limitless Options

But when I started looking at other products, my options were limitless. I could pick any item I wanted and try to sell it. I have sold a lot of different items over the years. I've sold the fundraiser chocolates, candy bars, potato chips, peanuts, trail mix, water, Monster energy drinks, cactus, fruits, hand sanitizer, and many more items.

I've had some that performed better than others, but I wouldn't have known this if I hadn't tested different products out.

One Staple Product

I recommend that you try to find one item that might perform the best in sales and stick to that as your main product.

How do you figure what your staple product should be? Well, the list of items I have sold before is a good place to start. Those are all good moving items. And of course, in the last chapter I will give the specific items I sold when we go over the exact blueprint of how I made $4,000 in 60 days.

Add A Second Product

Once you have your One staple product and the cash starts to flow in, you can start trying out additional items. When you add new items to test out, I'd say to try to stick to something similar.

For example, if you're selling honey roasted peanuts, then try cashews. Or if you're selling potato chips, then try something like Chex mix. You see how both of these examples are followed by something similar but different.

I'd recommend trying one new item at a time until you find one that sells well. This is especially recommended in the beginning until you start to get the hang of exactly what you're doing.

For the above example of the honey-roasted peanuts. I would have my staple product, the honey roasted peanuts, and then I would purchase 5 or 6 bags of cashews and try to sell them as well.

If I can sell those in a decent amount of time, then I would go ahead and purchase 10 to 12 bags and try it again. After that, I would just keep repeating the process until I am satisfied that they can perform consistently and make that my second product.

Now Add A Third Product

Once you've got the two different items selling, you can look to add a third, and then a fourth, and so on. But make sure you do the testing we spoke about at each step. In other words, try and test the third, then try and test the fourth, and so on.

Track Everything

Every good business tracks its sales and data and your business should be no different. I can't recommend enough to keep a log of all your sales.

You will want to write down your sales by item every day. Then you will want to write down what day and location your sales came from. The reason you want to do this is to not only test the products you are selling, but to test where you are selling them at too.

As the days pass by you won't always remember what locations are best for selling. Let's say you sell at three different locations but only two of them have customers that buy from you. You will want to know which one to avoid because it may just be a waste of time going there. This way you can replace that location with another one and then test it too.

Look At The Data

Writing down or tracking the information is only half the work. You will need to look at the information daily to make sure you are selling the right product at the right place.

Since you will most likely not be selling hundreds of different products, tracking only a few items doesn't take a lot of time. You will need to look at this information to see what items are selling the best. If you see an item that sells more than another, perhaps you should stock more of that item.

Determine How Much To Keep In Stock

How to use this information to determine how much of an item you should keep in stock. For example, if you see that you are averaging 60 sales a day of one particular item but only 12 of another, you now know which item to keep more of. You will need to keep a minimum of 60 of the first one.

Bonus Tip For Stocking

I'd honestly recommend keeping at least 2 days' worth of product when stocking, so that would mean 120 instead of 60.

The reason for this is that sometimes the items you purchase can run out of stock from where you buy them. This way you will have a little extra product just in case they run out and it gives the store time to get it back in stock.

Why Does The Store Always Run Out Of My Product

Sometimes you will find that stores will run out of the products you are selling quickly. This is because they may only normally sell 10 to 20 of these items a week. However, you may sell 60 to 100 or more each day. So, with this in mind, when the store you primarily buy your products from gets some in stock, you may need to buy everything they have.

I have sometimes spent more than $300 when they get an item I sell very well in on their truck. When you do this, they will be out until their next delivery, but at least you will have some. You will also want to try to find other stores that carry the same items that you can use as backup suppliers.

Don't Be Afraid To Reach Out

Another thing that you can do is to reach out to the manager of the store that you are primarily purchasing your product from. If you let them know what you are doing, and they can see what you've done so far, sometimes they can order additional products to keep in stock for you. But you may need to purchase from them for at least a few weeks for them to take you seriously.

On the other hand, it usually takes a store about 6 to 8 weeks for their system to identify the increase in sales. And at that point, they will most likely start carrying more of the item that you're selling automatically.

Chapter 6 Questions

1) When you explore new products, what kind of options will you have?

2) What is a staple product?

3) What should you do before you add a new product?

4) What do you need to do with the data?

5) What should you do if your primary purchasing location (store) runs out of product?

CHAPTER 7: TAKE ACTION NOW

"Information + Application = Transformation"

--CALEB MADDIX

Well congratulations, you have now finished learning about the main parts to start on your journey as an entrepreneur. Because I feel that it's so important, in this chapter we're going to cover what's called taking action.

The reason for this is because you can learn all about becoming an entrepreneur and starting your own business but unless you take action and use it, you'll never accomplish anything.

So, before we show you the blueprint that I used to make $4000 in 60 days. We're going to get you ready to take action on this blueprint as soon as you're done reading it.

Degrees Of Action

Most people fail to take action. If they do take action, they fail to estimate how much action to take. This is what you need to become a professional at. If you can learn to become a professional at taking action, you will no doubt have a lot of success in your future. Just the fact that you are reading this book will give you an advantage, but without action, you will not get far.

Sales Training Expert Grant Cardone speaks about this in his book *The 10X Rule*, that there are 4 degrees of action.

The First Action

The first degree of action is No Action. This is as easy as it sounds. It means you take no action towards it. It would be like reading this book, learning the skills to create a successful future for yourself, and then not doing any of the stuff you learned.

The Second Action

The second degree of action is that you Retreat. The idea here that you back away from whatever it is you learned to do. This is essentially the same as no action.

The Third Action

The third degree of action is you take Normal Action. Grant says this is the most dangerous action you can take. You are taking action and you think the action you are taking is good or normal. Normal will not get you ahead in life. This will get you what everyone else has. This is not what we are here to teach you, to be normal. We want you to be Extraordinary.

The Fourth Action

The fourth degree of action is Massive Action! This is the zone that you need to be in. In this level of action, it means that you are giving it your all. That you are 100% committed and out there hustling like nobody else. It means while your friends are out playing or hanging out, you're out pushing and working towards your goals.

Pay The Price

Grant has a saying about this idea, "Pay the price today, so you can pay any price tomorrow". This is going to be the difference between you becoming an entrepreneur or just an employee. There is nothing wrong with being an employee, most businesses need them. But it's so much better Owning the company, instead of working for the company.

Well, I don't want to make this chapter too long. I want you to be equipped with some knowledge about taking action. Hopefully, you are pumped up and excited about the journey that you are about to begin. I know I'm excited for you and I hope you have so much success that you can't imagine being anything but an entrepreneur.

My Recommendations For You

Once you've finished reading our book, I have 2 book recommendations to help you on your journey to success.

First, I recommend that you read Grant Cardone's *The 10X Rule*. This book will teach you how to become a master at taking Massive Action.

Second, I recommend reading *Keys to Success for Kids* from Caleb Maddix. At the time of this writing, Caleb is 18 years old and is already an 8-figure millionaire. He wrote his first book at 12 years old and has studied success his entire life. He has been an inspiration to me and helped me get to where I'm at today.

Chapter 7 Questions

1) What is it that Most people Fail to do?

2) What are the 4 Degrees of Action?

3) Which is the Most Dangerous Action? And why?

4) What does "Pay the price" mean to you?

5) What is the desired degree of action called? And why is it the best place to be?

CHAPTER 8: STEP BY STEP BLUEPRINT

"The single biggest financial mistake I've made was not thinking big enough. I encourage you to go for more than a million. There is no shortage of money on this planet, only a shortage of people thinking big enough."

--GRANT CARDONE

Well, here we are, the last chapter of *The Teens Guide to Starting Your Own Business: Your Step by Step Blueprint to Becoming a Teen Entrepreneur.* You are about to learn the Exact Blueprint of How I Made $4,000 in 60 Days. The same blueprint that will help you become a Teen Entrepreneur and Start Your First Business. I've tried to keep the blueprint simple and easy to follow so that you can duplicate it and use it yourself.

Remember that I can't guarantee that you will have the same success that I've had with it. However, I believe that if you follow this blueprint you should have no problems with duplicating it. You may need to make certain decisions about the products you sell if you see something is selling better than what it did in my experience.

Step 1

Here is our starting step. On the left side of the page you will find the directions of what you need to do. At the end of each step, we will track how much accumulated money you have saved and how much money you have made in sales after the step was completed.

Initial investment: Use $30, or if you have no money borrow $30.

Purchase: Go to Dollar Tree and buy $30 worth of the $1 Peanut MM's theater candies (the one that comes in the yellow box).

Sell: At your chosen location, sell them for $3 each.

Sales: Your sales from this step will be $90.

> **Total Savings after completing step 1:** $0
> **Total Sales after completing step 1:** $90

Step 2

After you have sold everything from the Step 1, you will now continue to Step 2.

Initial investment: If you used a $30 loan go ahead and pay it back now.

Profit: Your remaining balance from the previous step is $60.

Reinvest: All the $60 back into the product.

Purchase: $30 worth of Peanut MM's and $30 worth of Regular MM's (theater candies).

Sell: At you chosen location, sell them for $3 each again.

Sales: Your sales from this step is $180.

> **Total Savings after completing step 2:** $0
> **Total Sales after completing step 2:** $270

Step 3

Use your sales data to determine if one item sells better than the other. I have found that Peanut MM's usually sell better and I'm going to assume that for this step.

Profit: $180 from Step 2's sales

Reinvest: All $180 into more product.

Purchase: $120 of Peanut MM's and $60 of Regular MM's.

Sell: At your chosen location, for $3 each.

Sales: Your Sales from this step is $540.

Sourcing Tip: At this point, it may start getting harder to source your products. If you have more than one Dollar Tree around that helps, but it may not be enough. I would recommend starting to test out more products at this point. The next product I would add is the Sour Patch Kids Watermelon flavor. I always had a lot of success with this flavor.

Total Savings after completing step 3: $0
Total Sales after completing step 3: $810

◆ ◆ ◆

Step 4

At this step, you are making enough profit that we are going to add more money for reinvesting, and we're going to start saving some of the profit for your goals.

Profit: $540

Save: Move $240 into your Goal Money Fund.

Reinvest: $300

Purchase: $120 of Peanut MM's, $60 of Regular MM's, and $120 of Sour Patch Kids.

Sell: At your chosen location, for $3 each.

Sales: $900

Total Savings after completing step 4: $240

Total Sales after completing step 4: $1,710

Step 5

At this point, it is a good idea to start testing even more candies out. So, we are adding $60 to test more products.

Profit: $900

Save: $540

Reinvest: $360

Purchase: $120 of Peanut MM's, $120 of Sour Patch Kids, $60 of Regular MM's, and use $60 to test other products.

Sell: At your chosen location, for $3 each.

Sales: $1,080

Total Savings after completing step 5: $780
Total Sales after completing step 5: $2,790

Step 6

After your testing in the previous step, you are going to pick your best selling test item and move forward with it.

Profit: $1,080

Save: $720

Reinvest: $360

Purchase: $120 of Peanut MM's, $120 of Sour Patch Kids, $60 of Regular MM's and $60 of your bestselling test item.

Sell: At your chosen location, for $3 each.

Sales: $1,080

Total Savings after completing step 6: $1,500
Total Sales after completing step 6: $3,870

◆ ◆ ◆

Step 7

We are not going to be making any other adjustments here in the book. You will need to look at your sales data and determine if you should adjust any of the amounts of products you are buying.

Profit: $1,080

Save: $720

Reinvest: $360

Purchase: $120 of Peanut MM's, $120 of Sour Patch Kids, $60 of Regular MM's and $60 of your bestseller.

Sell: At your chosen location, for $3 each.

Sales: $1,080

Total Savings after completing step 7: $2,220
Total Sales after completing step 7: $4,950

◆ ◆ ◆

Step 8

Continue same purchases unless your sales data shows you should do it differently.

Profit: $1,080

Save: $720

Reinvest: $360

Purchase: $120 of Peanut MM's, $120 of Sour Patch Kids, $60 of Regular MM's and $60 of your bestseller.

Sell: At your chosen location, for $3 each.

Sales: $1,080

Total Savings after completing step 8: $2,940
Total Sales after completing step 8: $6,030

◆ ◆ ◆

Step 9

Continue same purchases unless your sales data shows you should do it differently.

Profit: $1,080

Save: $720

Reinvest: $360

Purchase: $120 of Peanut MM's, $120 of Sour Patch Kids, $60 of Regular MM's and $60 of your bestseller.

Sell: At your chosen location, for $3 each.

Sales: $1,080

> **Total Savings after completing step 9:** $3,660
> **Total Sales after completing step 9:** $7,110

◆ ◆ ◆

Step 10

Profit: $1,080

Save: $1,080

> **That's It!** This was the last step of this blueprint! After you have sold the items from Step 9 you have passed your goal of making $4,000!

Your Grand Total in **Savings** is: $4,740
And Your **Total Sales** are: $7,110

Final Thoughts

I just want to leave you with one final thought and that is Action. You have all the tools to get this done. However, without action, nothing will happen or change. You are at a point in your life where you can learn how to become successful.

You need to take Massive Action now to create a better life for yourself and your family. A life where you don't have to worry about money. A life that you are in control of as an entrepreneur and not an employee.

You are starting your first business here and the skills you learn now will help you down the road when you start a second business, or third or fourth.

So good luck with your business. If you have any questions you can reach out to us at sellingforkids.com

Here's The One Dollar Startup Method

I said I will show you how to get your startup capital with only one dollar. After reading the blueprint it should be obvious, but we'll cover it right now.

Use $1 and purchase 1 box of Peanut MM's from Dollar Tree. Resell for $3.

Use the $3 you made and buy 3 boxes of Peanut MM's.

Resell for $3 each.

Use the $9 you made and buy 9 boxes of Peanut MM's.
Resell for $3 each.

Use the $27 you just made and purchase 27 boxes of Peanut MM's.
Resell for $3 again.

Use $50 to buy 50 boxes of MM's.
Save $31.
Resell for $3 each.

Your total sales are now $150
And you still have $31 saved.

Your startup capital for the lawnmowing service is complete. But you could also keep going and just start the blueprint business model instead of the lawnmowing service.

Whatever you choose to do, We wish you good luck!

Chapter 8 Questions

1) Do you understand how the Blueprint works? Can you explain it to someone else?

2) Can you make adjustments to it? Why is data important?

3) If you have any questions about it, who can you ask? Or where can you go?

4) How quickly do you think you could make $4,000 yourself? More or Less than 60 days?

5) What do you need to "Take" in order to make this work?

SIGN UP FOR THE SELLING FOR KIDS NEWSLETTER

Stay up to date on our New Releases, Deals and More by signing up to our mailing list!

Sign Up Here >> SellingForKids.com

When you sign up for our Selling for Kids newsletter. We give you access to exclusive deals and offers, Advance Reader copies of our books, plus lots of tips, tricks and training to help you on your journey into entrepreneurship.

ABOUT THE AUTHOR

Tanya Rogers

Tanya Rogers is a 17-year-old author, entrepreneur, blogger, content creator, podcaster, and a high school senior. Along with her family, Tanya has dedicated their time to creating the Selling for Kids Book Series to inspire and teach future young entrepreneurs how to start their own business. Their primary focus has been teaching an easy and inexpensive method for kids and teens to start their first business.

She's created two blogs for education and finance. She also runs a podcast where she talks about business-related topics and tips to achieve mental health. Plus, she's co-writer with other authors on the Chang'E Project, a non-profit feminist organization dedicated to breaking down gender-based stigmas and improve women's education.

ABOUT THE AUTHOR

David Rogers

David Rogers is an entrepreneur, author, trainer and public speaker. David has been in the business of sales for almost 30 years and dedicates a lot of his time to training.

David, along with his daughter Tanya, and son Ethan have dedicated their time to creating the Selling for Kids Book Series as a way to help inspire and teach future entrepreneurs on how they can start their own business. Their main focus has been on teaching a method that is both inexpensive and easy to start for kids and teens.

BOOKS IN THIS SERIES

SELLING FOR KIDS BOOK SERIES

Selling for Kids The Book Series was created to help teach and inspire a future generation of young entrepreneurs.

The Kids Guide To Selling: How I Was Able To Make $4,000 In 60 Days

In our first book, The Kids Guide to Selling, we teach you about the nine fundamental principles you need to know to start your first business. Plus, you learn what you need to do Right Now to start selling and generating an income, following our simple and inexpensive business model.

The Teens Guide To Starting Your Own Business: Your Step By Step Blueprint To Becoming A Teen Entrepreneur

In our second book, The Teens Guide to Starting Your Own Business, we dig even deeper into the concepts of starting your own business and becoming a teen entrepreneur. Plus, we give you the step-by-step Blueprint of what, when, and how you need to do to launch your first business successfully.

The Teens Guide To Becoming An Entrepreneur: 102 Ways That You Can Start To Think Like A Successful Entrepreneur

In our third book, we will take your knowledge and skills to the next level by introducing you to the idea of creating the Entrepreneur's Mindset. We will be showing you 102 ways that you can start to think like a successful entrepreneur.

The Teens Guide To Mastering Sales: How You Need To Think To Become Successful At Selling

In the Teens Guide to Mastering Sales, we will show you how you need to think to become a master at selling. Your ability to sell, persuade, or convince others is a critical key to having success in business or life.

FOLLOW US

You Can Stay Up To Date

Instagram: instagram.com/sellingforkids

Facebook: facebook.com/sellingforkids

Amazon (Tanya): amazon.com/author/tanyarogers

Amazon (David): amazon.com/author/daverogers

Website: sellingforkids.com

www.ingramcontent.com/pod-product-compliance
Lightning Source LLC
Chambersburg PA
CBHW031543210526
45464CB00003B/1122